The Biblical Perspective of Finances

Prevailing views of finances.

God's view, which is really the only one that matters. First, it all belongs to God. He is the one who said that the world is His AND the fullness thereof. He said he owned all the gold, all the silver and the cattle on a thousand hills belonged to Him. True, there are multi-billionaires, but they pale in significance to Him who sits on the throne.

Adam sold his rights to the devil in the garden and Satan became the ruler of this world. Isn't it amazing that since God created the world and all that is in it, and actually owns it all, that the devil claims the right to the title, ruler of this world? The reason is that Adam sold that right.

Christians are to have dominion in the world. God gave Adam dominion in the garden.
Christians are to be stewards over all God's creation. As stewards we have an awesome responsibility to guard the environment as well as to be stewards over all God's creation. It is sad that many Christians are living far below their God given right by not claiming their rightful inheritance.

We are heirs and joint-heirs with Jesus Christ! That is one awesome responsibility and one that every Christian should exercise. Are you aware that all of this wealth that has been created by men is being laid up for the righteous? It is true. God is holding it for us Christians just waiting on us to wake up and take control.

So, if we can get it into our minds and our spirits that it all belongs to God and that we are His heirs along with the Lord Jesus Christ and can put all of this in perspective, we are poised to take on the greatest mission the world has ever seen. Can you imagine what can happen when we open God's treasury and begin to take our rightful place as stewards?

So grasp this concept and begin to take your rightful place in the Kingdom of God. It all belongs to HIM!

Then there is man's view. Man's view is simple also…it all belongs to him. The motto of the world is to get all you can, and can all you get! Man and his needs is the only thing that matters. It does not matter how many people you have to step on to get what you want, it all belongs to you, so go for it. Lie, cheat and steal…it doesn't matter as it is all yours, a nice juicy apple just waiting to be plucked. Man knows what is best for him.

He knows what he needs and wants. He knows how to get it. It's not just what you know, it's who you know. Push and shove, use every person you can to get what you want. It's called OPM…other people's money…so get it. It all belongs to man. That's what we are taught in school, that's what the world says and we have come to believe it.

So, take the money and run. Eat, drink and be merry for tomorrow we die. Get all the gusto…go for it. You can make it. It only cost a little more to go first class. All these are expressions we hear every day. Everyone's doing it. It's ok to cheat on your taxes. It's ok to cook the books, because that's man's view of money.

What is Stewardship? What is work ethic? Don't hear much about that nowadays. We think nothing of calling in sick. We can't wait until five. We have worker's rights. We are entitled. After all, isn't there a thing called entitlement? The government owes me. The company owes me. My parents owe me. After all, I am entitled!

When Adam sinned in the garden, God said that he would now live by the sweat of his brow. Man could no longer lounge in the garden and relax by the pool. He had to get out the hoe and start digging. Man has come up with some pretty ingenious ways of avoiding work.

But the fact is God gave him the responsibility of maintaining the Garden of Eden. He was given dominion over all the earth, over every beast, over every bird, over every fish; God placed it all under his hands. But with the fall, Adam sold that right to the devil.

> **GIVING GOD WHAT BELONGS TO HIM**
> The tithe is Holy unto the Lord. The first Fruits of our labor belong to Him. By paying Our tithe, we open the windows of heaven.
>
> **LETTING THE BLESSING POUR**
> In Malachi 3 we learn that by tithing we Open the windows of heaven. By giving, the Blessings are poured out. The amount of The offering determines the amount of The blessing.

TITHING AND GIVING ARE THE MEANS OF PROPOGATING THE KINGDOM OF GOD

1. God has ordained that the Church should be the depository of His Kingdom. It is after all, God's church (Matthew 16:18).

2. It is simple and fair (I Cor 16:2).

What is debt?

1. **When you owe someone money, <u>you are in debt!</u>**

    A. In strictest sense, secured debt is not debt.
    B. Collateral is property pledged or given for a loan.
    C. $5, $500, or $5,000, it's all debt.
    D. Collateral can be a TV set or a TV station!

2. **Debt is:**

    A. Any amount of cash you borrow without putting up collateral
    B. Any credit extended to you.
    C. Any service you take without paying for it at the time of receipt.
    D. Debt is a noun…never a verb…"to debt."

3. **Types of "debting"**

    A. Compulsive debting - repeated spending despite the pain it causes.
    B. Problem debting - compulsive debting in the making.
    C. Reasonable debting - Are your debts a problem?

4. **What do the Scriptures say about debt?**

"The borrower is the slave to the lender." Proverbs 22:7 TLV

"The wicked borrow and do not repay." Psalm 37:21

"Give everyone what you owe him: if you owe taxes, pay taxes; if revenue, then revenue; if respect, then respect; if honor, then honor. Let no debt remain outstanding, except the continuing debt to love one another..." Romans 13:7-8.

A problem...Who, Me?

1. **Where am I?**

    A. 3 positions on debt:
    - Overwhelmed by debt.
    - Concerned and worried that we are in over our heads.
    - Surplus of money and never worry about it.

2. **Am I alone?**

    A. 20 Million Americans are overwhelmed, a paycheck from disaster.
    B. Consumer debt is a staggering 78% of personal income!
    C. Credit card indebtedness jumped from $60 Billion in 1980 to $280 Billion in 1990.
    D. In 1986 personal bankruptcy rose 35%.
    E. Some earn over $100,000 and some earn less than $10,000 annually.
    F. Some owe hundreds of thousands and some owe only $500 or less.
    G. **BUT,** debt is debt!

3. **How serious is my problem?**

    A. Do you only pay the minimum on your credit card?

    B. Are your installments past due?

    C. Are your charge cards maxed out?

    D. Do you use your credit card for groceries or cash advances?

    E. Are you unable to pay insurance bills and taxes?

    F. Do you "rotate" bills with creditors?

    G. Do you work 2nd job to pay bills?

    H. Has your credit card been refused because you are maxed out?

4. **What's the worst it can get?**

    A. No debtors prison today.

    B. Judgment

    C. Garnishment

    D. Bankruptcy

5. Help! I need help!

    A. Non-profit credit counselors
(make sure they are non-profit)

    B. Many churches have counseling services.

    C. You can negotiate with each creditor and work out a payment plan.

HOW WE GET THERE.

1. **Repeated debt results from distorted attitudes about money and self.**

2. **What is money?**

    A. Simply:
    1. You give your employer work...he gives you money.

    2. You give a retailer money...he gives you goods.

    B. Mood changer.

    1. When the going gets tough, the tough goes shopping!

    2. Life owes me!

    3. I'm not worth much.

    C. Spending for status is a high dive into the pool of red ink.

    D. Money is neutral...neither good or bad.

    E. You can build a church or a death camp with it.

3. **Waiting for the Big Fix.**

   A. Get an inheritance

   B. Win the Lottery

   C. Make a big sale.

Problem is, it seldom arrives and when it does it doesn't fix anything!

THE WINDS OF CHANGE

1. **One Day at a Time**

    A. Today, one day, do NOT incur any new debt!

    B. That's easy. Just one day.

    C. Do not borrow $5 from a friend.

    D. Do not accept a service you plan to pay for later.

    E. Do not take out a loan from the bank.

    F. Do not use your credit cards.

    G. Just today. Don't worry about tomorrow…just today.

    H. You will never get out of debt by borrowing more money.

    I. Thousands of others have done it. I am no different. I can do it. I AM doing it. I AM doing it NOW!

    J. Review every purchase. Do I HAVE to have this. If not, don't get it!

    K. Brown bag instead of buying your lunch.

L. Break your piggy bank for groceries.

M. Sell any stock or bond even if you take a loss. Use it for groceries.

N. Sell some furniture, art or silverware.

O. Stay home & watch TV instead of going to a movie.

A. You must know exactly where your money is going. You will be surprised.

B. Buy a little note book at the store for 29 cents.

C. Keep it in your pocket or purse.

D. Mark down EVERY item you spend, for newspaper, groceries, snacks…EVERYTHING!

E. Keep a record for one month. Don't give up!

F. The record is useless if it is not complete. Keep it faithfully.

3. **The Weekly record**
   July 1 - 7
   Rent
   Groceries
   Clothes
   Entertainment
   Laundry
   Medical
   Telephone
   Transportation
4. **The Monthly Record**

SPENDING RECORD FOR JULY

WEEK	1	2	3	4	TOTAL
RENT					
FOOD					
CLOTHES					
ENTERTAIN					
UTILITIES					
LAUNDRY					
MEDICAL					
PAPERS & MAG					
TELEPHONE					
TRANSPORTATION					
OTHER					
TOTALS					

A. Break down Food Category by groceries, fast food, restaurants, etc.

B. Categories. Don't have too many or too few. Here are examples

Alimony
Books
Cabs/Limos
Car (gas, tires, repairs, insurance, car wash)
Contributions (tithes, offerings, gifts)
Child support
Children's expenses
Clothes
Cosmetics
Diners/Fast Food
Dry Cleaning
Education
Entertainment (movies, theater, concerts, circus, etc)
Utilities (Gas/Electricity/Water)
Gifts
Groceries
Haircuts/Beauty shop
Health Club
Hobbies
Home Equipment (appliances, dishes, pots & ans, tools, etc)
Home furnishings (tables, chairs, beds, rugs, etc)
Home repair (lawn, heating, plumbing, etc)

Home supplies (dish & laundry soap, toilet paper, etc)
House cleaning
Income taxes
Investments
Laundry
Legal expenses
Life insurance
Magazines/Newspapers
Medical (doctor, dentist, prescriptions, glasses, etc)
Medical insurance
Personal care (soap, shampoo, perfume, razor blades, etc)
Personal Growth (lectures, seminars, training courses, etc)
Professional Dues
Property Taxes
Public Transportation
Rent/Mortgage
Restaurants
Restaurants (paying for someone else's meals)
Sports
Telephone
Therapy
Tips/Gratuities
Tuition
Union Dues
Vacation/Travel
Vitamins
Misc. (if more than $20 you need to break it down more).

CREDIT CARDS...TO BE, OR NOT TO BE?

1. Carrying a credit card is like carrying a hand grenade!

    Why I <u>Have</u> to have a credit card:

    A. To rent a car

    B. To avoid carrying cash

    C. For identification

    D. To make purchases over the phone

    E. For business reasons

    F. In case of emergencies

    G. It makes life easier

Let's analyze them:

It makes life easier: Of course it does. You may have to think without one! It is very simple to live without a credit card. Try it.

I have to have one to rent a car. First, if you have to rent them that much your company should provide a company credit card for you. Second, you **CAN** rent a car without one, contrary to what you have been told. How do I know? Ask me. Most companies will take cash deposit between $150 - $400, depending on the length of rental. You should call ahead to verify.

I need it for identification. Bologna! 99% of places will use your driver's license.

I don't want to carry cash. How many times have you been robbed? How many times have you lost your wallet? You don't have to carry thousands in cash, if so, do it with traveler's checks.

I need one for business reasons. Bologna! Usually a card is used for entertaining. You can use cash. If you entertain often, use a company credit card.

I need it for emergencies. Nuclear attack? Riot or civil disorder? Maybe you will wake up penniless, hungry, and all alone. Happens all the time!!

Is a credit card ever justified? Yep! Here are the rules:

1. Keep it in a drawer. Do not carry it with you, unless you know you're going to use it.

2. Know exactly what you are going to use it for before you take it.

3. Use it for NOTHING except the intended purpose.

4. Return the card IMMEDIATELY on returning home.

5. Write a check immediately for the purchase or service.

The Budget

1. **Should be referred to as the spending plan.**

    A. Budget comes from Old French *Bougette*

    B. *Bougette* comes from *Bouge*, a small purse.

    C. Budgets are depressing

    D. Budgets seldom work for long

    E. What is needed is a Spending Plan

    F. The Spending Plan is just an expansion on The Spending Record.

SPENDING RECORD FOR MONTH OF _____, 20_.

	Week 1	2	3	4	Actual
RENT					765
GROCERIES					200
BOOKS					20
PUBLIC TRAN					30
CHILD SUPP					200
CLOTHES					65
CONTRIBUTION					200
PAYMENTS					300
DINER/FAST FOOD					75
UTILITIES					200
ENTERTAIN					50
HOUSE EQUIP					25
HOUSE FURNISH					25
HOUSE SUPPLIES					30
LAUNDRY					10
READING					20
MEDICAL					100
HOSP INS					200
MISC					15
PERSONAL CARE					40
RESTAURANTS					35
TELEPHONE					45
TOTALS					

The spending plan should be an objective with goals.

    A. Don't start a savings account until you are out of debt.

    B. Why pay 20% for a credit card and get 5% at the bank??

    C. Cut spending! Understand that treating yourself to dinner could mean adding an additional 2 months to payment plan!

    D. Instant gratification versus Delayed gratification

    E. If you buy $2,000 worth of furniture on a credit card, and only pay the minimum payment it will take you 31 years and 2 months to pay it off at 20% interest! That is $8,202 in interest!!

BUYING A NEW CAR

1. **<u>Don't!</u> A new car loses 50% of its value in 2 years!**

    A. Borrow as little as possible. If possible, save the money before a major purchase. Put as much cash down as you possibly can.

    B. Borrow the money for as short of time as possible. If you can afford the payments, make it for 24 months. Never longer than 3 years or the car will be worn out LONG before it is paid off. Then, when you to go to purchase again, the dealer will tell you that you are "Upside down." You owe $5,000 and the car is worth $1,000!

    C. NEVER buy "Credit Life Insurance" It is the most costly insurance in the market. If you need more insurance, buy Term Insurance (see section on Life Insurance).

    D. NEVER buy "Extended Warranties." Only the dealer benefits. Most problems will occur during the normal period provided in the manufacturer's warranty (Most drive train components will usually run over 100,000 miles).

NEVER buy after market products (rust protection, etc). Nearly all new cars come from the factory with rust protection. Do not have the dealer add radios, etc. You can buy them much cheaper locally.

> F. Don't buy a larger car than you need. While it is nice to have the extra room, remember the insurance will be higher and the gas mileage will be less.
>
> G. Don't buy gadgets that you won't use. Cellular phones can be purchased much cheaper from local phone companies.
>
> H. Buying vs. leasing? If you are in business and use it exclusively for business, maybe. If not, DON'T lease.

INSURANCE...PROTECTING WHO?

1. **Who needs it?**

    A. Insurance was designed to provide income for a family when the bread winner dies.

    B. Single people do NOT need life insurance

    C. Children should ONLY be insured for burial expenses.

    D. Wives should also ONLY be insured for burial expenses.

    E. Fathers should be insured for a comfortable income until the children are grown, then a modest income for the wife should she need it.

    F. When you have a proper savings structure, NO ONE needs insurance!

    G. Example. If you income is $40,000 per year, you should multiply that by 10, making $400,000 the policy amount. If that is invested drawing 10%, your family will have the salary replaced WITHOUT touching the policy amount!

H. What type of insurance do I need?
   Simple Term Insurance.

I. Under no circumstances should you spend money for "Whole Life," or "Cash Value" insurance. You will do far better by putting the money in savings.

J. Hospitalization Insurance - most have it through their employment. If not, check into insurance for the self employed. If you cannot afford this, take some kind of catastrophic insurance so that if there is a major medical problem you won't be wiped out.

K. Home owners insurance - if you are buying a home, the mortgage company will REQUIRE it and will generally factor that into the payments. If you are renting, you should have renters insurance if at all possible.

L. Auto insurance - most states require that you at least have liability insurance. If you car is old and is not worth more than $1,500 or so, don't carry anything but liability.

TO RENT OR NOT TO RENT, THAT IS THE QUESTION

1. **Real Estate has become a good investment again.**

    A. With the exception of the last few years, real estate has performed as good as most investments.

    B. You have to live somewhere, so you may as well be building savings in a home.

    C. You receive tax write off for all mortgage interest.

2. **How do I do it?**

    A. Several government agencies have low cost houses, especially for first time buyers (example HUD).

    B. You must decide on what type home you need (single family, condominium, zero lot).

    C. Where do you want to live?

    D. How much payment can I afford?

E. Use an agent or not? Depends. If you don't you can save several hundred or thousand dollars in commissions. BUT, do you have the time to do the research. Have you checked on loans? Do you have an attorney who can do title search, etc.

F. Types of financing: Seller Financing, Assumable Financing, Lease to own, Conventional.

G. Types of mortgages: Fixed Rate & Adjustable rate

H. 15 Year or 30 Year mortgage?

I. Must I pay points? A point is equal to 1% of the amount borrowed. If you plan to stay for a long time, pay extra points and less interest rate.

J. Title Insurance. YES! This means that if there is a lien discovered on the property, the insurance company pays it. This is what the title search does.

GETTING OUT!

1. Out of debt, once and for all.

A. Prioritize your bills. Example: You have a visa card with $500 balance and payments of $25. Divide 500 by 25 and you get 20. You have a Master Card with $800 balance and payments are $50. So, divide 800 by 50 and you get 16. Do this with each of your bills. The lowest numbers take the priorities.

B. Set your *accelerator* rate. If you can pay an extra $100 each month, add that to the payment of the first priority. Example: You pay $125 per month for 4 months and your Visa card is paid off, instead of 20 months! Now, take the $125 per month and pay the Master card and it is paid off in only 7 months. Then take the $175 you were paying for the Master Card and Visa and apply that to your next one. Keep on doing that until you **ARE OUT OF DEBT!!!**

C. By the time you get to your car and house payments, you will have an impressive amount to pay them off.

D. It is important that you contact your creditors immediately and tell them what you are doing. Most will be glad to work with you. If you find they will not, then you need to turn to a Credit Counseling service.

E. You must be totally honest with yourself and with your creditors.

F. Keep a record of all calls to and from any creditors. Record the date, time and what was discussed. This will remind you and will serve as a powerful tool in the event one of your creditors decides to take you to court. Judges are not real happy when people are trying to do their best and the creditor won't work with them.

SEA MONSTERS

1. **We are going to draw a map of where they are.**

    A. **Customer Account department.** Contact each one you owe and attempt to work out an amended payment if you cannot pay the full amount. Key word here is **contact.**

    B. **Collection agencies**. When the creditor cannot collect from you they will probably turn the account over to a collection agency. They will charge between 20 - 50% to collect the bill. Their tactics are never pleasant. They may intimidate and even threaten you. This is why it is important to contact the Accounting department before this happens.

    C. **The IRS.** You can bet they WILL collect their money. Contrary to what you may have been told, they will work with you to make payments on any taxes owed. The secret is; **TALK TO THEM!**

D. **Judgments.** If for any reason a creditor files a judgment on you and you are summoned to court, by all means GO to court, especially if you have been trying to work with the creditor. Here's some things to prepare you:

- Document your income and expenses
- Document your total debt structure
- Bring your repayment plan
- Bring your contact log where you recorded your calls
- State your commitment to pay the bill off
- Explain that you are in the process of trying to get out of debt.

Chances are you will come out with flying colors and no court costs

E. **The Credit Rating.** It is nearly an object of worship to some! Actually, there is no credit rating, just a credit report. Each prospective creditor will look at it with different views and ratings.

F. **Credit Score.** Varies, but that is what the creditors go by more than anything else. Several factors come into play here. The higher the score, the less the risk for the creditor.

"Keel the Bool."

"A poor Spanish peasant goes an old story, returns to his tiny hut where there is not even firewood. His wife and son are huddled under a blanket eating the last crumbs of bread. He tells them that men from the city wish to buy their bull to fight in the bullring. 'Oh no!' cries the boy. 'Not the bool. Not my favorite thing in the whole world, not my friend. Not the bool I raised from a little calf!'

'But, my son,' says the peasant, 'we have no money left and nothing to eat. They will pay us $20,000 for him. We can move to a house. You will have shoes, a bicycle. You will be able to go to movies, to go to school, to have all the things you never had before.' '$20,000?' the boy asks? 'Yes, my son/'

'Shoes? A bicycle? School?'

'Everything my son.'

After a moment, the boy replies 'Keel the bool!'

O.K., we've "keeled the bool." We've struggled and survived and paid off all our bills. Now, let's start the prosperous living part! Ready? Here we go.

INVESTMENTS

1. **Invest it all!**

    A. Think about it. All the money you've been paying for cars and houses and credit cards can now be put to work for you!

    B. Where should I NOT put my money?…in the Bank!

    C. O.K., so where? Here's some examples:

    - **Time Share Units** - The very worst possible investment! Don't.

    - **Penny Stocks** - Stocks selling for less than $5 per share. Generally, they are poor risks.

    - **Commodities** - If you are brave, have a stomach of iron, and have time to watch it, go for it. Otherwise, STAY AWAY!

    - **Rare Coins** - You had better know what you are doing!

    - **Collectibles** - Don't buy unless you like the collectable you are buying. Don't buy it for an investment, buy it because you enjoy it You had better know what you are doing.

- **Jewelry** - Like collectibles, buy it if you like it and want to wear it. Usually is not a good investment and you can lose your shirt if you don't know what you are doing.

- **CD's** - while offering a safe investment, usually do not keep up with inflation, so you are actually losing money!

- **Mutual Funds** - probably one of the best investments in the market.

2. **What is a mutual fund?**

    A. Mutual funds began in Europe early in the 19th Century.

    B. They began in the U.S. in 1924.

    C. They are a fund "mutually" created by a group of people who have "pooled" their money to buy stock.

    D. Mutual funds are generally managed by someone who is very experienced and trained in the money markets. Far better than you can do yourself.

    E. The main advantage is diversification. All your money is spread safely around in different companies.

F. Actually, the government forbids a mutual fund from investing more than 5% of its ssets in a single company.

G. The mutual fund does the paper work for you. They buy and sell and send you statements of how your money is growing.

3. **What types of mutual funds are there?**

   A. Open-End Funds can sell shares to the public as long as people are willing to buy them. They can grow as large as they can sell.

   B. Closed-End Funds issue a specific, limited number of shares. These shares are then traded like stocks, on exchanges, and their value –from day to day—is determined by marketplace supply and demand.

4. **Load or no load?**

   A. Load funds add the commission to your purchase. The commission can be up to 8.5%. Funds charging 7.25% - 8.5% are called *full load* funds. Funds charging 3%- 5% are called *mid-load* funds. Funds not charging a commission are called *No Load* funds.

5. **Fund categories**

   A. **Stock Funds** are mutual funds that buy stock in other companies.

   B. **Stock and Bond Funds** are often referred to as *balanced funds*, and they split their holdings between stocks and bonds.

   C. **Specialty Funds** include *Sector Funds*, which usually invest in one industry, such as technology, or gold stocks, health care, etc.

   D. **Bond Funds** usually invest in Government bonds. The danger is that if interest rates increase, they lose 10% of their market value by every point of interest the Prime Rate increases! They can be risky.

   E. **Money Market Funds** usually invest in short-term IOU's from banks and the strongest U.S. Corporations. They usually pay higher rates than most other funds.

BANKRUPTCY...THE EASY WAY OUT?

1. **Bankruptcy laws were enacted in the U.S. in 1841.**

    A. Prior to this you went to debtor's prison!

    B. Now Bankruptcy is less humiliating

2. **Types of Bankruptcy**

    A. **Chapter 7** - Discharging of debts. This should not be used by Christians unless your situation is truly hopeless and there is no way you can pay your bills.

    B. **Chapter 13** - reorganization. This allows the repayment of most debts under more favorable terms. All collection against you is stopped. This usually takes 3 to 5 years.

3. **Bankruptcy is not the answer**

    A. Bankruptcy stays on your record for 10 years. Even after that, you will be asked if you have ever filed bankruptcy.

    B. There are things that are not exempt from the bankruptcy laws:

Alimony, Child support, and Taxes. None of these are reduced.

"The wicked borrow and do not repay." Psalm 37:21

ESTATE PLANNING

1. **Death is the destiny of every man." Ecclesiastes 7:2**

    A. Amazingly not every one plans for death. My dad always said; "Just dig a hole and put me in it." I had to pay off his bills when he died!

    B. **Wills** handle the distribution of assets. They appoint a guardian for minor children.

    C. When you die without a will, it is called "Dying intestate." The state then receives your assets and appoints a guardian for your children!

    D. **Living Trusts** - There are 3 advantages:

    They avoid the probate process

    They avoid conservatorship

    They save taxes

    E. A "Revocable" Living trust can be changed or terminated. Don't ever make an irrevocable trust.

F. The Living trust is primarily for people having a total estate of $600,000 or more, but can be used with assets of less.

RETIREMENT...THE GOLDEN YEARS?

1. **Will Social Security be secure?**

    A. Even the government admits that unless drastic action is taken, Social Security will be bankrupt no later than 2010.

    B. Social Security was never intended to be your sole means of retirement, but only a supplement.

    C. 87% of Americans are retiring in poverty! Most companies have a retirement plan. Use it!

2. **Tax Deferred Retirement Plans**

    A. 401-K   Employee Pension - Profit Sharing Plan

    B. 403-B   Non-Profit Organization Plan

    C. IRA   Individual Retirement Account

    D. Keogh   Proprietorship, Partnership Plan

    E. SEP   Self Employed Plan

3. **How much do I need to retire?**

   A. You will probably need 75% of what your present salary is. So, if you are making $40,000 per year now, you will need $30,000 when you retire. How long do you expect to live after you retire? Multiply that by the number of years and you have how much you need!

4. **Where does the money come from?**

Component	**Source**
Social Security	U.S. Government
Pension	Employer
Distributions	IRA
Distributions	Annuity
Interest & Dividends	Savings & Securities
Rental Income	Real Estate

Table of Contents

Cover Page

Table of Contents

Course Outline

Bibliography

The Biblical perspective of finances

What t is debt?

A Problem. Who, Me?

How we get there

The winds of change

Credit cards. To be, or not to be

The Budget

Buying a new car

Insurance…protecting who?

To rent or not to rent. That is the question

Getting out!

Sea monsters

"Keel the Bool!

Investments

Bankruptcy…the easy way out?

Estate planning

Retirement, the Golden Years?

www.ingramcontent.com/pod-product-compliance
Lightning Source LLC
Chambersburg PA
CBHW061520180526
45171CB00001B/266